Paris Beauty

Rich Hebron

Paris
Beauty

Rich Hebron

Books by Rich Hebron

Homeless but Human
Primary Ponderings

Nuance & Notes Series

Chicago Clarity
Paris Beauty
New York Energy
Los Angeles Dreams
Miami Magic
Milwaukee Sensibility
Mexico City Merriness
London Happening

Written by Rich Hebron
Illustrated by Kenneth Ferguson

Milly Moves to the Farm
The Boy and the Rocketship

Rich Edition Classics

The Great Gatsby

Rich Hebron is an American author. He has lived half his life in Chicago and the other half on a farm in rural Wisconsin. He fuses these backgrounds together to draw inspiration and live a meaningful life in a world accelerated by the internet and digital technology. He hosts the Rich Conversations Podcast where he explores self-development and talks with friends in art and science fields.

Connect with Rich: @richhebron

Blue Byron Books
bluebyronbooks.com
Chicago, Illinois

Writing & Art: Rich Hebron, richhebron.com
Editing: Autumn Hebron
Contributors: Annie Tran, Joe Anhalt

Printed in the United States of America.

ISBN 978-1-966742-02-9 (paperback)
ISBN 978-1-966742-03-6 (e-book)

For those who want to create a beautiful life

Author's Note

My first near-death experience happened on the farm. An oil line blew on the tractor and became engulfed in flames. I jumped from it. My second near-death experience occurred four years afterwards. This time, three men pointed Uzi guns at my face, threatening to shoot me. Fortunately, it was just another reminder that life will end—all our lives. So how do we want ours to be?

After initially going fast, with the adrenaline from the encounter lasting months, I decided to stop. The difference between speed and velocity is that velocity is speed in a direction. Anyone can go fast—especially in circles. But it takes skill and something deeper to channel energy with purpose. Refining purpose requires restarting at the beginning. Be open and see what's happening. Pursue curiosity and, above all, patience.

My curiosity led me to hotel lobbies. I spent time visiting different ones in downtown Chicago and just sat, observed, and wrote notes, often sipping espresso or red wine. An appreciation for details developed. Gratitude followed. Every thing was there for a reason. Nothing was a coincidence. The creators of the spaces aimed to evoke particular emotions and feelings in people. They staged a vibe.

I learned that design affects our mind and influences our culture. The whole of something is the result of individual things. From a pencil to a house. From a shoe to our cities. From a light fixture to our lives. The story of our life is the result of every individual decision we make. The universe is the result of every individual atom.

Beauty is the result of those small, individual components. Love is understanding those small, individual components.

My passion and appreciation for detail expanded from hotel lobbies to virtually everything in life and in people. But something I especially had fun with was observing the designs on building facades. My favorites were those resembling nature. They possessed the character I aspire to be: dynamic, flexible, playful, and fruitful. Things that are alive are adaptable. Things that are dead are stiff, rigid, and brittle. Since human beings are part of nature, the same is true for people and their ideas and perspectives.

I encourage you to reflect on the follow questions:

- *Are current environments failing to design nuance?*
- *If design affects culture, what are the ramifications of prioritizing cheap and fast?*
- *Is a society that ignores patience a healthy one?*
- *If individuality is abandoned, is Love too?*

This is a series called *Nuance & Notes*.
This is a book of nuance of Paris with notes from my mind and observations in the world.

Paris is a city that makes a person feel in love or alone. It stands out as one of the most thoughtful and intentional cities in the world. An aura permeates the culture to where any scene from the eye appears artistic and purposeful, whether mundane or extraordinary. The city possesses a cohesion and oneness in its aesthetic that demands a higher level of effort while remaining playful and carefree. Paris doesn't take itself seriously but is also the most serious about how things should look and be. It's a rare city that uses bad weather to enhance its charm and romantic appeal. There's little argument over the fact that Paris is beautiful.

Shot on iPhone 13 Mini

The world isn't black and white
The world is gray
Our life will be more beautiful
if we accept this and navigate the gray

It's all a matter of our mind
Our experience in and of life
is a reflection of it

Many people simply want
the ability to be open
without judgment

Reliability is the greatest skill
Be sure our actions match our words

Sit in silence
It's the superpower of the 21st century

Rich Hebron

We can come together
on fundamental values

Nature's interconnectedness
is beautiful
We're beautiful

Understand what is essential
We'll live a fulfilled life

The fresh crisp air helps clear the mind
It's a beautiful wonder

Be open and understand
Be subjective and objective

Life is more beautiful
if our mind is present in each moment

Let's take one breath in
Let's take one breath out

Be less antagonistic
Be more helpful

Take a step back
It will reveal its self

If we are all one,
we each need to feel loved

How's our energy?
Let's do our best to keep it high,
so we can give it to others

Beware of the perception
our initital reaction has on our mind
It's powerful

We're an individual in a
collective of individuals
The more Love each of us exhibit
the more Love the collective will be

To give space is to give love
To give love is to give space

Give our self less things to think about
Then let's prioritize those things

Where do we give our attention?
Be conscious

If we're free to live how we want,
we should ask how we want to live
Together

It's not about going every where
It's not possible to go every where
Know where we want to go
It's possible to go there

At first sight,
remove Fear like a cancer to the body
It's fatal

Consider our strengths
Water the seeds accordingly

Do nothing
Observe
React

Prioritize peace of mind
Nonmaterial affects material

The health of a being
depends on energy

It'll be easy for us to grow together
if we're giving our best from our self

To give our self
and accept the outcome
is beautiful

The more people the more energy
It's electric

Our future together is bright
It gives us so much energy

Is there a collective conscience
of a crowd?

Thinking small is a waste of energy
unless it's a component

Living as our self is courageous

Patience is a rare commodity
Our presence will be highly valuable
if we're patient

Let's approach each day
with a good attitude and positivity
Our quality of life depends on it

We shouldn't hate any thing
Hate is Fear
Be open to learn about what we hate
We may grow

Breathe
Relax

More people move through Love
than through Fear

Lighting affects our energy
as human beings

Practice gratitude
It's an easy way for us to return
to the right state of mind

Remain calm
Excitement can cause adverse effects
Let's not overreact

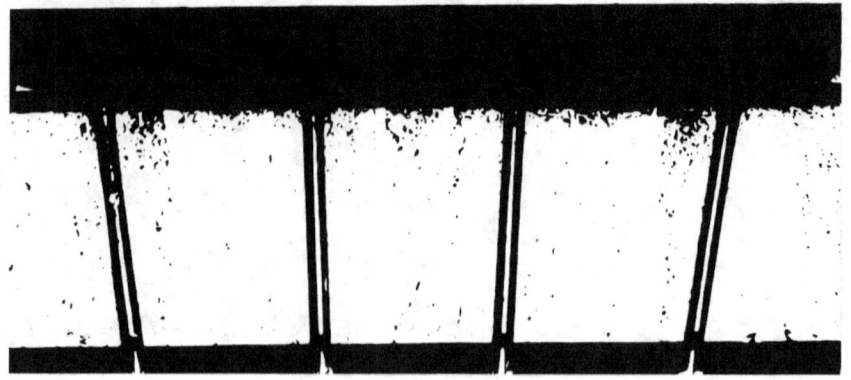

Take care of the small things,
so they don't become great
Take care of the small things,
so they become great

Peace is not something to strive for
Peace is
Remove the unnecessary

Things that are alive are flexible
Things that are dead break

Paris Beauty

People mirror their environments
Environments mirror their people

Don't force our ideas onto others
Let's live our ideas
and provoke curiosity in others

Fires are the end of something
Fires are the beginning of something

Understand or assign
our purpose in the world
We can find peace by living it
Be bold

We can serve others
to lighten the collective burden
If we don't serve others,
we add to our individual burden
as well as the collective burden

Rich Hebron

If we're in a hurry, we're lost

If we possess hate, we're off balance
Identify the source of Fear
Take action on it

The four needs of human beings are
water, food, shelter,
and human connection

If we can think,
we can be grateful
Isn't this wonderful?

A healthy balance of
idealism and pragmatism
is the recipe for what we crave

We are not what we say
We are what we do

Rich Hebron

Our friends teach us much of life
Be open and grateful
Celebrate them like we would our self

Let's use our phone
the way our ancestors used a stone
Our phone is a tool

We can solve most of our problems
by going for a walk

Some days are nothing to us
Some days are everything to us
What we keep on our mind
determines the meaning

What is will be
unless there's a change in our habits

The ability to understand
and consider context separates
the conscious and not conscious

What is in our control?
What is not in our control?
Our fate is paralysis
if we cannot answer this

If we know the difference
between being and trying,
we know happiness

What are we willing
to wake before dawn for?
In our answer lies direction
moving forward in our life

Like our ancestors
we can only do one thing at a time

Is this natural?
Or is this unnatural?
Answer and make decisions

Start at the ending
Then start at the beginning

Let's focus on our similarities
before our differences
with others

Become clear before action
Velocity over speed

Giving our time is kindness
Kindness is beautiful

Let's compliment others more
It'll give us practice
in appreciating the details in life

Don't spend so much time in our head
that we miss the nuance around us
We'll likely find beauty in nuance

Breathe
Clear our mind
Observe what is happening
React accordingly

Eye contact is important

Willpower is cute
Habits are effective

Generosity is beautiful
Give more kindness
Become more beautiful

Let's have more
questions than opinions

Rich Hebron

We're one part of a bigger ecosystem
The healthier we are,
the healthier we all are

Breathing negativity
will poison our body

Time is short
Love is real

We would be better if we asked for help
Help is waiting to be asked

Rich Hebron

Imagine our self on a stage
Live as the role we play

Human beings are meant to be
in nature
or with each other

Rich Hebron

Keep our head up
otherwise we miss what's happening

Stage our self
in conducive environments
for the best energy

What are our collective habits?
Would we like to improve any?

Close our eyes and imagine
a space we feel loved in
Go there whenever we want

It'd be silly to be angry at the weather

When did we lose our playfulness?
Go back out there and have fun

We tend to have the most fun
when we play

How can we find more time for play?

Act with awareness

Do we believe that people
are influenced by their environments?
If so, let's create great environments

What environment are we in?

Where do we want to be?
If it's not here then where?

Rich Hebron

Overthinking paralyzes

If we think trendy,
do we know our self?

Fun is contagious

We are energized for our life
It's interesting and inspiring

Know the rivers to swim upstream in
Know the rivers to swim downstream in

Imagine the wonder of lightning
before human beings understood it

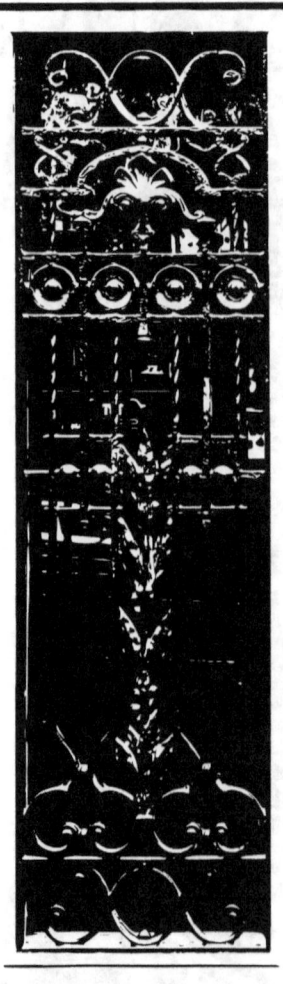

In nature,
the most beautiful and enduring
are adaptable

Our reaction to what happens
is our choice

Rich Hebron

Give our love to the nuances in life

Are we having fun?
Our answer is a signal
either way

Patience is beautiful
Impatience is ugly

Try less
Be more

A beautiful being
doesn't need to say a word
Nuance is clear

Today is the same as yesterday
Tomorrow is the same as today
All is the same but will we be?

Does this deserve a reaction?
It may not

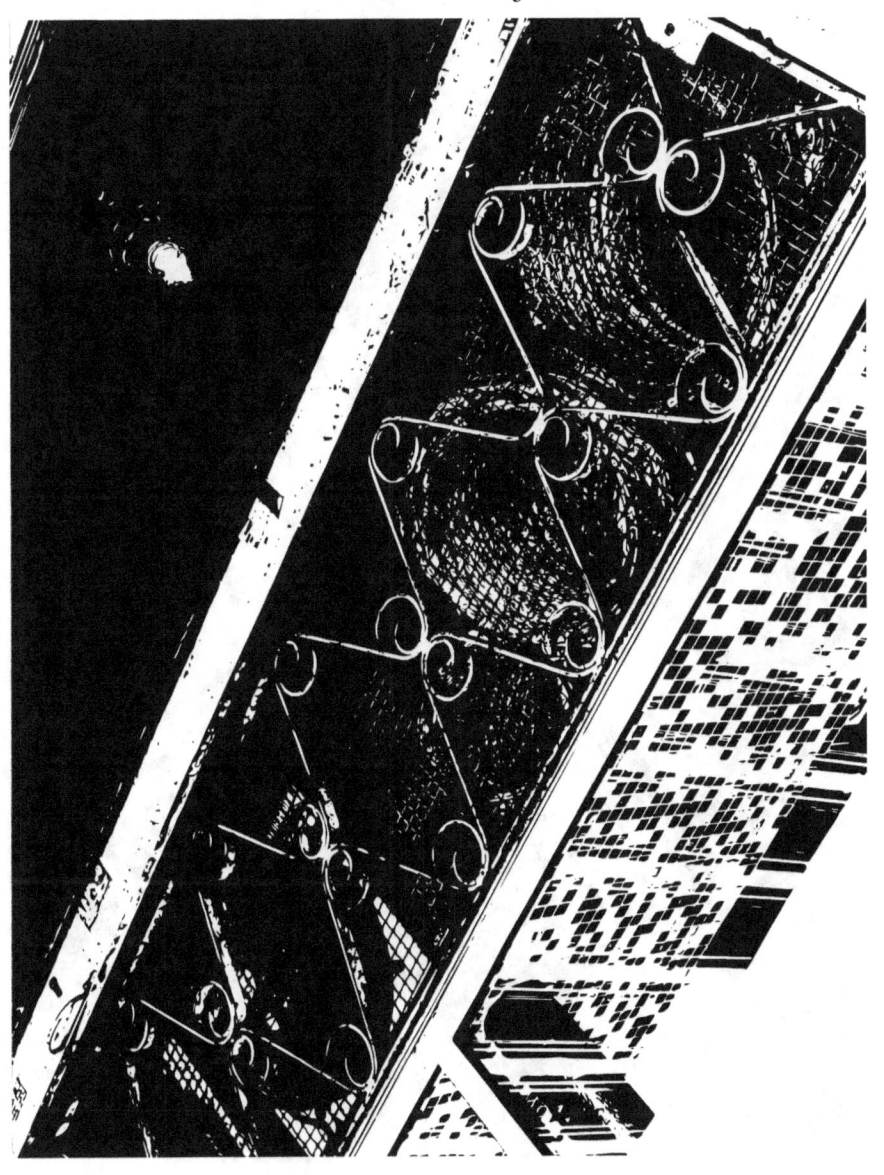

To be beautiful
pursue curiosity and continue learning
throughout our life

A bench has many stories

Let's develop the ability to see things
before they happen

Every thing
is right in front of us
See and act

What compels our self to sit down?

Surround our self with flowers
Laugh at anger

Is it the painting?
Is it to rest?
Is it because of boredom?

We must participate to
reduce loneliness and suffering
Be active

It's not a shame to ask for help
People will help us if we ask

Rich Hebron

Do important things
need to be written down?

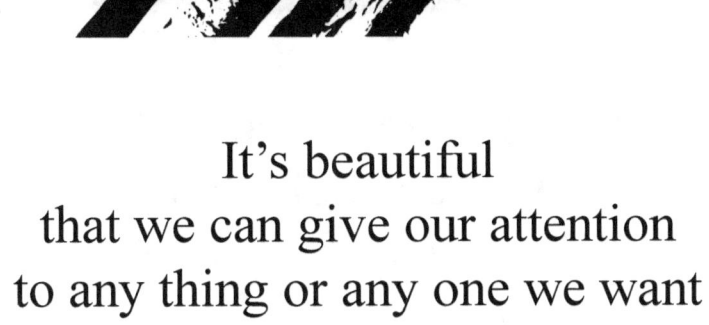

It's beautiful
that we can give our attention
to any thing or any one we want

Rich Hebron

If we can think of something,
we sure could do it
How beautiful is this?

Don't get ready
Stay ready

Our time is a gift
How will we share it?

The seasons
remind us of our gift of time

A Thought on Cities

Our cities are our greatest invention. They're the engines of civilization. Cities are the hubs that bring people, ideas, and opportunities together. They generate energy and inspire the pursuit of dreams and a better life.

I feel humans are meant to be isolated in nature or surrounded by other humans. Fusing the two maximizes energy and accelerates regenerative processes. This is why I shuffle between living on a farm in rural America and traveling to big international cities.

Having lived in Chicago for over 15 years, I am an enthusiastic advocate for urban living. I believe that the healthier the city, the more dynamic the society and culture. I'm passionate about exploring and analyzing the facets of each city. I believe in competition and that our cities should be constantly learning, adapting, evolving, and growing to serve and increase the quality of life for its residents. I love observing and comparing cities, noting their strengths and weaknesses, the effects of local geography, the movements and flows, and how every small matter contributes to the larger matter.

Cities are where big things happen. I believed this as a little kid growing up on a farm and I know it now as an adult who has experienced their impact.

I'm proud to combine notes that can help realize individual human potential with artwork that demonstrates the beauty collaboration can produce.

Rich leads weekly self-reflection sessions
to help people create more beautiful lives

Join in on the Rich Conversations Podcast
or visit the Rich Hebron YouTube channel

Connect with Rich: @richhebron

Notes

Notes

Notes

Notes